SNOWY DAYS

A First Look

PERCY LEED

Lerner Publications ◆ Minneapolis

Educator Toolbox

Reading books is a great way for kids to express what they're interested in. Before reading this title, ask the reader these questions:

What do you think this book is about? Look at the cover for clues.

What do you already know about snowy days?

What do you want to learn about snowy days?

Let's Read Together

Encourage the reader to use the pictures to understand the text.

Point out when the reader successfully sounds out a word.

Praise the reader for recognizing sight words such as *is* and *to*.

TABLE OF CONTENTS

Snowy Days. 4

Snowy Days

It is a snowy day.
The air is cold.

When it is snowy,
the sky looks white.

Snowflakes fall
to the ground.

7

When it is snowy,
animals leave tracks.

Plants freeze.

When it is snowy, snowflakes melt in our hands. Snow sticks to our hats.

Why doesn't snow melt on our hats?

When it is snowy, deer dig for food. Birds eat from bird feeders.

When it is snowy,
we wear warm clothes.

What do you
wear when it
is snowy?

14

We shovel the snow.

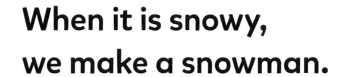

When it is snowy,
we make a snowman.

Have you ever been sledding?

We go sledding down hills.

When it is snowy,
we warm up by
the fire.

A snowy day is fun!

You Connect!

What is something you like about snowy days?

What have you noticed animals do in the snow?

What do you like to do on a snowy day?

STEM Snapshot

Encourage students to think and ask questions like a scientist! Ask the reader:

What is something you learned about snowy days?

What is something you noticed about snowy days in the pictures in this book?

What is something you still don't know about snowy days?

Photo Glossary

plants

shovel

snowflakes

tracks

Learn More

Murray, Julie. *Winter Weather*. Minneapolis: Abdo, 2022.

Peters, Katie. *The Snow Is Fun*. Minneapolis: Lerner Publications, 2020.

Salas, Laura Purdie. *Snack, Snooze, Skedaddle: How Animals Get Ready for Winter*. Minneapolis: Millbrook Press, 2019.

Index

Photo Acknowledgments

The images in this book are used with the permission of: © shironosov/iStockphoto, pp. 4–5; © XiXinXing/iStockphoto, p. 6; © PNPImages/Adobe Stock, pp. 7, 23; © Veronika Dvořáková/iStockphoto, pp. 8, 23; © Johnrob/iStockphoto, pp. 9, 23; © Marilyn Nieves/iStockphoto, pp. 10–11; © Erik Mandre/Shutterstock Images, pp. 12–13; © John Hammann/iStockphoto, p. 13; © hobo_018/iStockphoto, p. 14; © Rossario/Shutterstock Images, pp. 15, 23; © XiXinXing/Shutterstock Images, p. 16; © FatCamera/iStockphoto, p. 17; © EduardSV/Shutterstock Images, pp. 18–19; © Air Images/Shutterstock Images, p. 20.

Cover Photograph: © Choreograph/iStockphoto

Design Elements: © Mighty Media, Inc.

Lerner Publications Company
An imprint of Lerner Publishing Group, Inc.
241 First Avenue North
Minneapolis, MN 55401 USA

For reading levels and more information, look up this title at www.lernerbooks.com.

Main body text set in Mikado a Medium.
Typeface provided by Hannes von Doehren.

Library of Congress Cataloging-in-Publication Data

Names: Leed, Percy, 1968–author.
Title: Snowy days : a first look / Percy Leed.
Description: Minneapolis : Lerner Publications, [2024] | Series: Read about weather. Read for a better world | Includes bibliographical references and index. | Audience: Ages 5–8 | Audience: Grades K–1 | Summary: "With winter comes snow, and with snow comes the cold. But that doesn't mean that snowy days can't be fun! Leveled text and full-color photographs support young readers while they learn about snowy days"–Provided by publisher.
Identifiers: LCCN 2023005525 (print) | LCCN 2023005526 (ebook) | ISBN 9798765608791 (lib. bdg.) | ISBN 9798765616789 (epub)
Subjects: LCSH: Snow–Juvenile literature. | Weather–Juvenile literature. | BISAC: JUVENILE NONFICTION / Science & Nature / Earth Sciences / Weather
Classification: LCC QC926.37 .L45 2024 (print) | LCC QC926.37 (ebook) | DDC 551.57/84–dc23/eng20230714

LC record available at https://lccn.loc.gov/2023005525
LC ebook record available at https://lccn.loc.gov/2023005526

Manufactured in the United States of America
1 – CG – 12/15/23